Cold World

The Aesthetics of Dejection
and the Politics
of Militant Dysphoria

First published by O Books, 2009
O Books is an imprint of John Hunt Publishing Ltd., The Bothy, Deershot Lodge, Park Lane, Ropley,
Hants, SO24 0BE, UK
office1@o-books.net
www.o-books.net

Distribution in:

UK and Europe
Orca Book Services
orders@orcabookservices.co.uk
Tel: 01202 665432 Fax: 01202 666219
Int. code (44)

USA and Canada
NBN
custserv@nbnbooks.com
Tel: 1 800 462 6420 Fax: 1 800 338 4550

Australia and New Zealand
Brumby Books
sales@brumbybooks.com.au
Tel: 61 3 9761 5535 Fax: 61 3 9761 7095

Far East (offices in Singapore, Thailand,
Hong Kong, Taiwan)
Pansing Distribution Pte Ltd
kemal@pansing.com
Tel: 65 6319 9939 Fax: 65 6462 5761

South Africa
Stephan Phillips (pty) Ltd
Email: orders@stephanphillips.com
Tel: 27 21 4489839 Telefax: 27 21 4479879

Text copyright Dominic Fox 2008

Design: Stuart Davies

ISBN: 978 1 84694 217 4

A CIP catalogue record for this book is available
from the British Library.

Printed by CPI Antony Rowe, Chippenham, Wiltshire

O Books operates a distinctive and ethical publishing philosophy in
all areas of its business, from its global network of authors to
production and worldwide distribution.

Cold World

The Aesthetics of Dejection
and the Politics
of Militant Dysphoria

Dominic Fox

BOOKS

Winchester, UK
Washington, USA

CONTENTS

In grateful memory of Julia,
who got me started

The Cold World

Sadness does something to the way we see the world. In the experience of deep sadness, the world itself seems altered in some way: coloured by sadness, or disfigured by it. Rather than living inside us, as our normal passions do, our sadness seems to envelop everything: we live inside it, as if it were a cocoon or a prison. At such times we seem particularly aware of the world *as* a world, as a place where we have to live. This awareness can become artistic or political: *artistic*, when the world made strange by our own detachment and dissociation presents itself as an object of fascination; *political* when the difficulty of going on living in such a world begins to reveal its causes in the impersonal circumstances of our personal sorrows.

Both kinds of awareness have their origins in desolation, in the sense that the world is frozen and that nothing new is possible. Both can lead to terrible paroxysms of destruction, attempts to shatter the carapace of reality and release the authentic self trapped within; but both can also lead away from the self altogether, towards new worldly commitments that recognise the urgent need to develop another logic of existence, another way of going on.

For most of this book we will be concerned with artistic productions: poetry, music, the novel. When we speak of "a world", we do not mean either the earth (which is singular: "*the* earth", the ground beneath our feet) or the globe (which is becoming-one, the goal of a "globalization" which seeks to rule on the compossibility of all possible worlds). We mean "a world" in roughly the sense in which one may speak of the world of a work of fiction; that is to say the way matters appear within the fiction, its image of the world.

In Malory's *Morte d'Arthur*, for example, a remarkably

self-contained and internally consistent world is first constructed and then violently dismantled. Malory's Arthurian world is the highly stylised world of a fable, a model universe defined by its invariants. Every battle scene in the *Morte d'Arthur* is practically identical to every other: the antagonists clash together like snorting bulls, shatter their spears, "void" their horses, unsheathe their swords and fight one another to a stand-still on foot. But the narrative moves towards the death of Arthur, the dissolution of the round table and the breaking of the code of chivalry: the end of the world of the fable, and the beginning of a world more recognizably "modern". Of course the fictional world is embedded in a "real" world, and refracts its self-image and preoccupations; but the import of the fiction is that the "real" world is also a transitory order of appearance: this too will pass.

Let us now take a musical example: "The White Birch", the third and final album by the now largely forgotten 1990s Sub Pop band Codeine. Codeine played a deeply mournful music, impressively slowly. When their original drummer left the band, they reputedly had great difficulty in auditioning for another who could play consistently at their speed. Most drummers would succumb sooner or later to the urge to inject some life into the proceedings by speeding up, getting louder or introducing additional flourishes and fills. (Drummers are not known for their asceticism). The dynamics of Codeine's music were the physics of its world: a world in the grip of entropy, in which everything is running down. The title of their first album, "Frigid Stars" captured both the glacial brilliance of Codeine's sound and – paradoxically for a collection of intensely introverted songs about failed and failing relationships – its cosmic scope.

By the time of the "The White Birch", Codeine's sound was not the heavy, space-filling drone of other slow-core bands, but a strangely enervated, plaintive chiming, in which each struck chord was allowed time to decay. The vocals were delivered in an adenoidal, Kermit-like croon; the lyrical themes were loss, exhaustion, draining anxiety and (as in "Tom", with its refrain "I'll throw sand in your eye, / you need a reason to cry") helpless spite. In spite of these unprepossessing characteristics, "The White Birch" builds towards moments of intense beauty and release, culminating in the transcendent final moments of the album's closing song "Smoking Room".

The lyrics of "Smoking Room" are typically minimal, consisting of a single quatrain followed by a couplet:

Spent afternoons
In the smoking room.
The things I said back then
Still make me burn with shame.

The world is frozen now.
It glitters, sparkles and shines.

The first quatrain seems to refer back to a time of leisurely self-indulgence and convivial warmth, whiled away in male sexist banter. Something has happened since to rob the shameless language of the smoking room of its enjoyment, so that it is now shameful to recall. The pleasure of shame-lessness depends on an initial sensitivity to shame, a sense that one is perhaps carrying things a bit too far, and in this case it appears that the shame has outlasted the pleasure by which it was initially masked or overridden.

The couplet, "The world is frozen now/it glitters, sparkles and shines", bears no immediately obvious relationship to the preceding quatrain, and is followed by a long instru-mental tail in which a repeated sequence of four chords, played by lightly striking rather than strumming the guitar strings, shimmers away into silence. But there is a metaphorical link between the two verses, which hinges on the juxtaposition – familiar from Renaissance verse – of burning and freezing. While "burning" signifies the intense emotion connected with past events and attitudes, "freezing" signifies the shift to detached aesthetic observation, a shift from the dynamic "I...back then" of personal reflection to the static "world...now" of the present.

One possible response to "Smoking Room" is to hear it as a dramatization of Codeine's rejection of rock music's vital machismo, turning away from its "smoking room" (or "locker room") ambience of exaggerated gestures and swaggering priapic boasting towards a dreary - yet fascinating - emotional terrain. In place of rock's all-conquering lust for life, Codeine's music enacts a stark resilience, pointing to the possibility of beauty, hope and love even when the libido is utterly depleted, when every imaginable material and emotional resource has been stripped away. In many respects, "The White Birch" is a painfully depressing album to listen to, but its final moments are both beautiful and consoling, opening out onto the glimmering "now" of a cosmos in suspended animation.

In the essays that follow, we will call this frozen constellation the "cold world": the world voided of both human warmth and metaphysical comfort. This cold world is the world made strange, a world that has ceased to be the "life-world" in which we are usually immersed and instead stands before us in a kind of lop-sided objectivity. It is a world between worlds, a disfigured world. We will show how the cold world can be both the theme of art and, as experience, one of the conditions under which artistic works may be composed. The first part of this book is concerned with this "aesthetics of dejection".

We will also consider the relationship between the world of dejection and that of the political militant, the person who has become separated from his or her world and turned against it, under the rubric of a "militant dysphoria" or politicised unpleasure. The later part of the book accordingly considers some fictions of adolescent and post-adolescent revolt, arguing that such revolt has a counter-factual component, embodying an intransigent will that the world be other than it is.

The cold world is the object of two exemplary modernist productions: T. S. Eliot's *The Waste Land*, and Samuel Beckett's *Endgame*. Let us briefly consider both. In *The Waste Land*, it appears that the world of European culture has lost its ability to cohere and has been reduced to fragments. It is no longer confidently able to know its own "mind", and is confronted with a desolate reality beyond the reach of cultural mastery: the desert of the real, "fear in a handful of dust". Dryness, desiccation, is the material condition of this world; the poem awaits a revivification in the form of "damp gusts bringing rain". There are thus two things lacking in the world of *The Waste Land*: a vital principle capable of knitting organic bodies together, and a hegemonic principle that can gather the threads of culture, enabling it to be properly mindful of itself.

By correlating these two lacks, so that the reduction of organic life to "dust" and of cultural life to "fragments" are viewed as symptoms of the same malaise, Eliot is able to place the crisis of European cultural mastery (of which the organised barbarities of the First World War might be considered the primary evidence) within an allegorical framework. Within this framework, cultural decline and resurgence can be represented as alternating, like "death" and "rebirth", according to the cyclic temporality of fertility myth. Just as the natural world passes through seasons,

5

spring following winter, so the life of a culture may also be subject to periods of hibernation and renewal. The allegory is ultimately political – it is about cultural power, and is intended to console and strengthen a threatened hegemony – but it works through a simultaneous spiritualization (through the turn to "mythic" time) and naturalization (through the assimilation of cultural "vitality" to organic life) of power.

In *Endgame*, by contrast, the world is not losing its mind but its contents: ordinary language survives the extinction of its referents, and in doing so ceases to be ordinary. The "coldness" of Beckett's world is not the coldness of dead matter, of a world that persists in spite of the loss of linguistic meaning, but the chill of the void around language, which achieves a stark lucidity once there is nothing or next to nothing left for it to be *about*. There is no question of a revival or resurgence in *Endgame*: what's gone is gone, but what is most terrible is that that which endures, endures. As Stephen Immerwahr sings, in Codeine's "Old Things": "Things don't last too long, / but when they do, / they last too long".

The cold world is the world in abeyance, in withdrawal, be it the ossified disaster zone of Anselm Kiefer's paintings or the festering cacotopia of William Burroughs's kicking junkie. It is the vitalist world fallen into inert matter, the animist world deserted by its presiding spirits, the heroic world overtaken by bourgeois commercialism – which, Marx claimed, "drowns the most heavenly ecstasies of religious fervor, of chivalrous enthusiasm, of philistine sentimentalism, in the icy water of egotistical calculation". Finally, it is the world of amorous occlusion, of love's failure or exhaustion.

In American Music Club's classic song of heartbreak "Western Sky", the songwriter Mark Eitzel declares that "the world's a shadow of what went before, / the world gives off

6

none of its own light". Here, the coldness of emotional disappointment and self-exile ("time for me to go away, / I don't belong in this place") is registered through the trope of illumination. The world of amorous enchantment, a cosmos knitted together by love, falls into shadow when the "light" of the other is withdrawn. This may seem like an example of "pathetic fallacy": the projection of an inner emotional state onto the indifferent canvas of external reality. But the world of the lover is indeed *a* world, an order of appearance with its own integral logic, albeit one fatally bound to the vicissitudes of a particular encounter. Indeed, Eitzel's claim, of the light of this world, that "you can still see it shining, / shining in the Western sky" asserts that whatever the fate of the amorous subject it engenders, the fire of love itself is eternal. Nothing in the subsequent experience of either person can finally invalidate the truth of the amorous encounter, no matter how occulted it may become.

The cold world imposes itself as final, terminal, because it is the termination of a world, its metaphorical freezing or blackening. Just as a given "life-world" is endowed with resources and qualities which make it possible to live well within it, so the experience of the cold world (or "unlife-world") is the experience of the exhaustion of these resources and the extinction of these qualities. This experience places in question the value of "the world", and with it the opposition between the mundane and the exceptional, the worldly and the unworldly. "The" world, thus disenchanted, is revealed as "a" world, a world among possible worlds; but it is also estranged from its conditions of possibility, to the extent that it seems scarcely credible that such a world could ever have existed at all.

For example, the narrative of "peak oil" identifies the cultural and technological co-ordinates of "advanced" societies as coterminous with the historically brief epoch, now drawing to a close, of copious and readily-accessible fossil fuel. The shock of the "peak oil" narrative is not only that it warns of a great and imminent crisis in these societies, but that it identifies their *world*, supported by a steadily unfolding narrative of social progress and technological advancement, as ephemeral and illusory, "unsustainable" and unsustained by any permanent reality. What the "peak oil" narrative declares (along with a brace of other ecological disaster-scenarios) is that "another world" is not only possible but inevitable, since this world cannot go on as it is (and, indeed, has in a sense already ended, inasmuch as its condition has already been diagnosed as terminal). To put it another way: not only is another world possible, but the present world is *impossible*: its very appearance is a kind of ontological mishap, a disorder in the real.

Let us now close this introduction by considering a fable of worldly enchantment and disenchantment: Iris Murdoch's *The Flight From The Enchanter*. In her introduction to the novel, the critic and novelist Patricia Duncker notes the "ghost of political commitment" which "haunts" its narrative. The cause of the band of "wealthy dinosaurs who were once the suffragettes" is a case in point. In a startling eruption of political vigour, the "dinosaurs" unexpectedly intervene in a shareholder's meeting to save their old radical paper, the *Artemis*, from purchase by the "enchanter" Mischa Fox through his proxy, the egregious Calvin Blick.

The paper is not what it was: it has become a literary periodical, run as a failing financial concern by the brother of Rosa Keepe, who had inherited shares in it from her mother. The preservation of the *Artemis* from the clutches of a male proprietor becomes a rallying point for the old suffragettes, but the very rationale of the cause is in dispute:

"I'm afraid," said the woman with the fringe, "that I find

it far from confusing. The prospective buyer is someone who is not, to put it mildly, a supporter of female emancipation. To consent to this sale would be to consent to change the character of the paper altogether."

"In fact," said Hunter, "the character of the paper has already changed. Since female emancipation has been achieved - "

"*What?*" said the lady in the mantilla. There was a general murmur.

"This young man is under the impression that women have been emancipated!" said someone at the back. There was a crescendo of voices.

"I confess I find this quite shocking!" said the woman with the fringe. "Why, the very fact that the phrase 'female emancipation' still has meaning for us proves that it has not yet been achieved."

Calvin, who had been turning boldly to study each of the speakers in turn, said suddenly, "Would you agree, madam, that the fact that the phrase 'emancipation of the serfs' is significant proves that the serfs are not yet emancipated?"

The Flight From The Enchanter, p. 173

The expression "female emancipation" carries a controversy within itself. It implies that the condition of women has hitherto been one of subordination to men, at least metaphorically comparable to that of slaves or serfs. Inasmuch as the opponents of female suffrage were those who did not accept this premise, part of the polemical force of the phrase lay in its power, in use, of distinguishing friend from foe. An opponent might have used the phrase mockingly, suspending it between quotation marks, but only a "supporter" would have used it in earnest. When the "woman with the fringe" says that the phrase "still has meaning *for us*", she means that its very use indicates a situation in which those for whom the phrase "has meaning" are pitted against those for whom it does not.

Calvin Blick's retort, that a phrase such as "emancipation of the serfs" may be "significant" without signifying that "the serfs are not yet emancipated", deliberately overlooks the polemical, partisan dimension of the phrase. It "is significant" ("one" knows what it means, or once meant) but no longer has meaning "for us", for the militant collectivity that takes the part of the not-yet-emancipated. What is at issue in this exchange is thus the normalization of a militant phrase intended to separate and polarise: its absorption into the language of the state, which has the ambition of being common to both friend and foe.

To say, as Hunter does, that "female emancipation has been achieved", is to regard the issue as having been settled by the granting of women's suffrage. It implies that the condition of women was never, in truth, one of thorough-going subordination to men: women merely lacked the vote, which has now been given to them. Everything else that the phase "female emancipation" might once have indicated is forgotten.

The "ghost of political commitment" shrouds itself with a form of words that has become anachronistic, a phrase that "is significant" in the language of general opinion but no longer has the polemical power to name the separation of the militant from that opinion. It has on the contrary become another name for the victory of the state over the militant: of the normal over the exceptional, of consensus over dissent. The brief and glorious revolt of the "dinosaurs" provides one of the novel's key reversals, but it is a moment of surreal anachronism rather than a rekindling of the flame of feminist rebellion (which, when eventually it came about, adopted the distinctly more modern-sounding name of "women's liberation").

Patricia Duncker observes that what the "dinosaurs" have going for them is "intelligence, intolerance and acumen", and that "their politics is not for the unworldly or the ironically disengaged". Yet they are plainly not creatures of the world in which they intervene, but of a world already declared obsolete: they emerge from political retirement, like King Arthur recalled from Avalon, in answer to a summons as enigmatic as it is compelling. Why, after all, does it matter whether or not the *Artemis* falls into the hands of the "enchanter", Mischa Fox? It ultimately matters because, in the world of *The Flight From The Enchanter*, Mischa Fox matters (we are never quite told why, or in what way); because he is "the enchanter", and the novel is a fable about the breaking of enchantment, and thus about the disfiguration of its own world.

For Duncker, "political commitment" and worldliness are to be opposed to ironic disengagement and unworldliness. To be politically engaged is to be engaged in and with the world, to wield an acumen that comes of being all too familiar with the wickedness of its ways:

> There are in fact only two kinds of people to whom unworldliness comes naturally: holy fools, or the arrogant and privileged. The former do not respect the kingdom of this world and the latter are so carefully protected from its realities that they do not need to understand it in order to survive...The poor, the vulnerable and the oppressed need to understand the mechanisms of power. Their lives depend upon that understanding. They are never unworldly.

Here, unworldliness is the province of the privileged, whom the world does not touch, and the "holy fool" who accepts worldly misfortune with equanimity. The struggle against injustice verifies with every blow struck or received that the world in which it is staged is the "real world", most inexorably real for those victims of injustice who need every ounce of their acumen to escape being crushed by it. Ironic disengagement, whatever its triumphs and its charms, is to be seen as a guilty turning away from this real world, a lapse of commitment. Just as to be worldly is to "understand the mechanisms of power", so to be unworldly is to be mystified, wilfully and complicitly unconscious of those mechanisms.

Let us now revisit our earlier assertion that the experience of the cold world brings the opposition between the worldly and the unworldly into question. In that experience, the world appears before us in a kind of disfigured objectivity. We are no longer fully immersed in it, or engaged with it; indeed, our habitual satisfactions and modes of engagement are suspended, placed beyond reach. It is at this moment, however, that the "mechanisms of power" truly become accessible to understanding. The experience of the cold world is one of dislocation, of eviction; of being eased or jiggled or jolted out of one's place in the world. One possible, and politically significant, consequence of this is that one's former position in the scheme of things may become apparent as a meeting-place of forces: one is separated, more or less forcefully, from what one had previously assumed and defended as one's "interests".

Iris Murdoch's novels arrange moral dislocations for their characters in order that those characters should discover significant parts of themselves to be the transitory forms taken by conflicts of custom and desire rather than emanations of a dependable intrinsic selfhood, an immortal conscience reliably directing their attitudes and actions. It is straightforward enough to act with integrity when one's decisions are circumstanced by dependable moral constraints. To be a principal character in a Murdoch novel, however, is more often than not to be thrown into a situation in which the maxims one has chosen to be bound by have ceased to be intelligible, in which one's principles are not so much put to the test as rendered nonsensical. The canniness of the worldly is routinely disarmed by the uncanniness of desire.

The rhetoric of worldliness emphasises the immediately situated character of political decision-making and action, against abstract or other-worldly considerations of principle. It inveighs against abstract moralism, utopianism and fantastic dreaming, the solipsistic cinema of revolt that plays endlessly in the private inner theatres of privileged would-be radicals. But a political situation is seldom immediately graspable in its concrete reality; it is rather "enworlded", materialised through a relational order of appearances, and it is with these appearances that – whatever the real stakes of the conflict – the actors in a political situation are often largely concerned.

Let us fix this "seldom" and this "often" to a condition: only at certain very rare moments, moments of profound disruption and severity, do mundane and quotidian calculations of interest, reckoning with the present world-order of values and appearances, give way to concrete decisions in the subjective path of a truth. Worldly realism knows nothing of truth; it is wholly absorbed in deliberating between greater and lesser "evils", which is to say that it moves entirely within corruption, employing corrupt means in the pursuit of corrupt ends. Such are the "mechanisms of power" with which we are encouraged to acquaint ourselves. The cold world is the world in which these mechanisms are shown to be incapable of upholding a truth, but to operate rather through a kind of generalised power of falsity. It is not the world is at really is, but the un-world in which "the thing which is not" stands exposed in its lack of being.

It is the inhabitant of the cold world, evicted from all home comforts and pressed "sheathe-and-shelterless" against the emptiness of being, who like the poet Gerard Manley Hopkins must find a way to recommence his existence, a new way to go on:

NOT, I'll not, carrion comfort, Despair, not feast on thee;
Not untwist - slack they may be - these last strands of man
In me ór, most weary, cry *I can no more*. I can;
Can something, hope, wish day come, not choose not to be.

Written In Blood

In the summer of 1885 the poet Gerard Manley Hopkins composed a series of "terrible sonnets", portraying a scarcely imaginable extremity of spiritual abjection. In these poems, which include "I wake and feel the fell of dark", "No worst, there is none" and "Carrion Comfort", the world Hopkins had once celebrated as "charged with the grandeur of God" is transformed into a "winter world" of depressive isolation, in which the ecstasies of religious devotion give way to an aching horror of existence:

> I am gall, I am heartburn. God's most deep decree
> Bitter would have me taste: my taste was me.

The Terrible Sonnets are commonly viewed as a type of confessional poetry or autobiographical self-portrait: they are read as depicting a state of mind of which they are also a by-product. Hopkins's biographer Robert Bernard Martin goes so far as to declare that "[i]f it can be said of any work of art, it is true that these are not poems about misery but the feeling itself...they are experiences so immediate that the reader constantly feels that they wholly possessed Hopkins at the very moment of their composition".

Martin's slightly hedging construction here ("if it can be said...") recalls Hopkins's own in the letter to Robert Bridges in which he wrote concerning the sonnets that "if ever anything was written in blood, one of these was". To write "in blood" is to set the substance of one's own life down on the page; the expression also implicitly likens the rigors of poetic composition to the anguish of Christ at Gethsemane, where he is said (in an image which now circulates as a general metaphor for intense exertion) to have sweated blood.

Whether or not they were truly "written in blood", and whether or not they are "the feeling itself" of misery transmuted into poetic form, it is true that the Terrible Sonnets do not merely treat misery as a theme, but bear in their very composition the trace of an intense mental anguish. Hopkins's image in "Spelt from Sybil's Leaves" of "a rack / Where selfwrung, selfstrung, sheathe-and-shelterless, thoughts against thoughts in groans grind" captures precisely the Terrible Sonnets' quality of setting thought grindingly against thought without "sheathe" or "shelter" of syntax to separate them. As Martin suggests, the nearest thing in English verse is the poetry of the Metaphysicals, with its abrupt juxtapositions of heterogeneous matter. Instead of the tranquil temporal flow of lyrical consciousness mulling over its recollections, there is an effect of stark simultaneity: each poem composes a fractured present.

Once again, we will speak of this fractured present as the "world" of the poems, and specifically as the "cold world" of disenchantment. Just as "[t]he world is charged with the grandeur of God" is a statement as much about the world as it is about the state of mind of the poet, so the bleak vista presented by the Terrible Sonnets is not merely an interior landscape but also an existential situation, opening out onto a dark constellation of which the suffering individual is only a part. Let us explore this constellation, starting with the sonnet which begins:

> No worst, there is none. Pitched past pitch of grief,
> More pangs will, schooled at fore-pangs, wilder wring.
> Comforter, where, where is your comforting?
> Mary, mother of us, where is your relief?

If Hopkins had written "no *worse*, there is none", this would have been readily intelligible as an expression of extremity: *this* is the worst, it doesn't get any worse than this. But to deny the existence of a *worst* is to say something different, akin to Edgar's aside in *King Lear* that "the worst is not, so long as we can say 'this is the worst'". Edgar's statement implies that the very worst is beyond the power of utterance: that dying, which brings an end to all utterance, is the worst thing that can happen. The worst and the naming of the worst cannot coincide. What Hopkins says, however, is that "the worst *is not*", without qualification: *there is none*. Even dying is not the worst; indeed, it may be only one in an infinite series of catalepses, turns from bad to worse. "No worst, there is none" is a metaphysical statement: it asserts the possibility of an unlimited intensification of anguish. As the demonically possessed Dr Weir declares in the space-horror movie *Event Horizon*: "hell is only a word. The reality is much, *much* worse".

For any merely mortal creature, there is a limit beyond which any worsening of its condition will result in its death: to be mortal is to be subject to a kind of "personal worst" which marks the limit of one's endurance. Hopkins's assertion that there is *no* worst must therefore be understood as pointing to something beyond his animal mortality. For him something worse and other than dying is possible, namely eternal suffering. To be the particular suffering creature that Hopkins is at the moment this cry is wrung from him is to have a foretaste of the pains of damnation ("[t]he lost are like this"), of which any taste whatsoever is always only a foretaste of worse to come: "more pangs will, schooled at fore-pangs, wilder wring". The sufferer might say, with Marlowe's Mephistopheles, "why this is hell, nor am I out of it".

It is difficult to know how one is to be comforted by the poem's closing instruction to "creep, / Wretch, under a comfort serves in a whirlwind: all / Life death does end, and each day dies in sleep", since the poem has already denied that death is the limit of suffering. The figural relationship between the death that ends "all / Life" and the sleep that ends "each day" suggests that death is like sleep as much as sleep is like death: a temporary "lull" or anaesthesia, without any power to arrest suffering for good. "*[E]ach* day" is by implication a day amongst other days, a member of a series; the end of one member of the series does not end the series, but rather enables it to continue. If "death" can be a name for the end of a day that will be followed by another day, if each day not only ends but "dies" in sleep, then the "death" that ends "all / Life" is clearly no guarantee of finality.

It appears, then, that the poem summons a threat that it cannot entirely banish or master: "Comforter, where, where is your comforting?" Not, certainly, in the closing cadence of this sonnet. The notion that "the worst" lies beyond the power of utterance paradoxically affirms that power: "we can say 'this is the worst'" precisely because our saying so forestalls the worst, places it at a symbolic remove. The worst that can be named is not the worst; thus, the ability of language to say "this is the worst" is the ability to say "the thing which is not": to negate that which is and to construct, in the domain of the symbolic, a counterfactual scenario. What "No worst, there is none" does is to refuse the comfort of the counterfactual: it does not rely on its own power of utterance to distance itself from the worst, but addresses itself to an abyss of suffering that voids all comforts.

The world into which Hopkins here finds himself "pitched past pitch of grief" is a kind of negative image of the world of "God's Grandeur", which is also a world in which intensities wrung from finite things ("like shining from shook foil", in one superlatively lovely phrase) ascend towards the infinite, "gather[ing] to a greatness, like the ooze of oil / Crushed". Even the works of men, inexorably bent towards finite ends, cannot fail to disclose God's grandeur even as they disguise it. At any moment, the creature's experience in this world may be one of identity with the blessed, or identity with the damned: not future expectation of damnation or salvation, but direct experience of the immanent reality of both. This direct experience – epiphanic in "God's Grandeur", cacotopic in the Terrible Sonnets – extinguishes the power of death, and reveals the creature to itself as immortal and faced at every moment with an eternal decision between two subjective paths.

Like Hopkins's "I wake and feel the fell of dark, not day", Philip Larkin's late poem "Aubade" begins with the speaker coming to dreadful consciousness in pre-dawn darkness:

I work all day, and get half-drunk at night.
Waking at four to soundless dark, I stare.
In time the curtain-edges will grow light.
Till then I see what's really always there:
Unresting death, a whole day nearer now,
Making all thought impossible but how
And where and when I shall myself die.
Arid interrogation: yet the dread
Of dying, and being dead,
Flashes afresh to hold and horrify.

To see "what's really always there" is to see nothing that one does not always see, but to be deprived of the ability to make-believe that it is not "really...there". Larkin's concern in "Aubade" is also with a failure of language, distributed between the rational apologetics of philosophy ("specious stuff") on the one hand and the "vast moth-eaten musical brocade" of religious consolation on the other. Neither is able to dispel the "special way of being afraid" that is the fear of having "nothing to think with, / nothing to love and link with". While philosophy calls on the capacity to "think" to dispel the fear of death, religious mythology employs the capacity to "love and link", to make life and death part of a web of meaning; but death for Larkin is precisely the destitution of both of these capacities.

It is not clear, however, that what Larkin is really afraid of is actually *death* as such. What really horrifies him is rather the thought of "dying, and *being dead*" (my italics). The condition he describes as mortally and implacably terrifying is neither one of non-being (which philosophy identifies as the destination of all mortal things), nor one of eternal suffering (which religion declares to be the immortal fate of those unreconciled with God), but rather one of permanently anaesthetised existence. Death is "the anaesthetic from which none come round", a radical privation of aesthetic sense: "no sight, no sound, / No touch or taste or smell".

It seems, then, that "[w]hat's really always there", what "stands plain as a wardrobe", is the un-aestheticised world of naked existence, the world as it exists apart from its counterfactual elaboration in language. This aesthetically denuded reality repudiates all attempts to rationally determine one's standing within it, or cover its nakedness with a pleasing "brocade" of mythology. "Death" for Larkin is then, in Paul de Man's useful phrase, "a displaced name for a linguistic predicament": a name for a failure of linguistic power that deprives the subject of the ability to make sense of, or take pleasure in, the world as it appears.

A common thread linking "I wake and feel the fell of dark" to both "God's Grandeur" and "No worst, there is none" is the metaphorization of sunrise and sunset. In "God's Grandeur", the setting of the sun prefigures its rising the following morning: the natural event serves within the poem as a metaphor for the supernatural comfort of the resurrection. To speak of a "natural event" in this context is already to speak paradoxically, however: it is the predictable regularity of the succession of sunset and sunrise that makes it the figure *par excellence* of natural consistency, of the cyclic and circadian "rhythms" of natural life. An "event" is, by definition, something other than the consistent recurrence of something already given (Beckett's "nothing new"). For Hopkins, however, the "natural" can be given the character of an "event" by being yoked, in a moment of epiphany, to the absolute novelty of divine creation. A sunrise may be at once the natural successor to a sunset, and the breaking upon the world of an entirely new dawn, that of the resurrection.

This "at once" is violently contradictory, and a major problem of Hopkins's verse is that of finding ways of stating this contradiction without succumbing to it. Be that as it may, given the metaphorical linkage "God's Grandeur" establishes between the breaking of *this* day and the dawn of Easter day, it is evident that to feel, upon waking, "the fell of dark, *not* day", is to wake into a world *without* novelty: a world upon which no new day has dawned, that is just as one left it when the previous day "die[d] in sleep". This is the world under the sway of the tyranny of "what's really always there": the cold world of existential horror.

By "existential horror", we mean the "special way of being afraid" that Larkin speaks of, a modality of terror that is linked to the very permanence of the real, the fact that it is *always* there. (Philip K. Dick once defined reality as "that which, when you stop believing in it, it doesn't go away"). This fear, which "flashes afresh" (like a demonic double of Hopkins's "shining from shook foil") from the very midst of things, has the power to both "hold and horrify". It is not only a fear *of* stasis, but a terror the experience of which *is* stasis, the experience of being held fast in place, frozen in the real. In old age Larkin, who had named a book of youthful poems "In the grip of light", found himself with increasing frequency in the grip of the grave. It is this seizure, this ek-stasis, which connects the rare moments of epiphany in Larkin (as in his description of the "any-angled light" which he imagined would "congregate endlessly" in an uplifted glass of water) with his susceptibility to terrible irruptions of dread. Like the world of the Parousia, ablaze with grace, the cold world voided of divine presence is capable of inspiring fear and trembling: a terrible, immobilizing awe.

Hopkins's "winter world" is the termination of the world of messianic hope: the forsaken world, of which Christ's crucifixion, rather than his triumphant entry as Messiah into Jerusalem, represents the final truth. This final truth is realised in the "I am" of "I wake and feel the fell of dark": "I am gall, I am heartburn; God's most deep decree / Bitter would have me taste; my taste was me". The "I" of the poem is here identified with the vinegar and gall offered to the crucified Christ, and with Christ himself tasting the bitterness of death. The Christian disciple, the follower of Christ, is – as both the Christian tradition and anti-Christian polemics have abundantly remarked - the inheritor of this bitterness. But does the galling bleakness of the Terrible Sonnets announce the possibility of another world besides that sustained by theodicy and messianic expectation?

Hopkins's late poem "That Nature is a Heraclitean Fire, and of the comfort of the Resurrection" announces a new (or rather, very ancient) schema of the natural. In this poem, nature is presented as radical inconsistency, continuous change, rather than cyclic consistency and homeostatic order:

Cloud-puffball, torn tufts, tossed pillows | flaunt forth, then chevy on an air-
    Built thoroughfare: heaven-roysterers, in gay-gangs |

22

they throng; they glitter in marches.
Down roughcast, down dazzling whitewash |
wherever an elm arches,
Shivelights and shadowtackle in long | lashes lace,
lance, and pair.

This is the world of the multitude, of the throng in which
identity is separated from itself, coming into being and
passing away according to the currents of the "air- / Built
thoroughfare" that is its natural element. The resurrection
here is not a supernatural event shattering the order of the
natural world, but the fulfilment of its deepest inward
tendency towards self-renewal. "God's Grandeur" had
already spoken of "the dearest freshness deep down things",
but this "grandeur" remains latent, a charge accumulating
secretly in the well of being rather than manifested in its
most superficial phenomenality.

If in "I wake and feel" Hopkins had identified with the
crucified Christ, in "That Nature is a Heraclitean Fire" the
identification is reversed:

In a flash, at a trumpet crash,
I am all at once what Christ is | since he was what I
am, and
This Jack, joke, poor potsherd, | patch, matchwood,
immortal diamond,
Is immortal diamond,

Christ is able to effect the resurrection of even the most
downcast of beings, the materially destitute "Jack, joke, poor
potsherd", precisely because "he was what I am". The
confusion of tenses and pronouns here does not establish an
identity persisting through time and space, uniting the
"Christ" and the "I" of the poem in a common history, but

rather the collapse of spatio-temporal distinction - "I am *all at once* what Christ is".- and with it of separate identity.

The repetition of "immortal diamond" at the end of the poem is initially puzzling, but in fact the key to the poem lies in the minimal difference between the two occurrences of the phrase. In its first appearance, it completes the sequence: "Jack, joke, poor potsherd", etc. As discarded pots fragment to potsherds, so fabrics fray to shreds and patches and wood splinters to "matchwood". These are the remnants which lie buried in earth waiting to be uncovered by archeology, undergoing a continual process of reduction which strips them of their form. The "immortal diamond" formed under great pressure deep below the earth's surface represents the limit-point of this subterranean transformation: the most deeply buried organic matter becomes at last this hard and glittering thing, disinterred by volcanic eruptions. Death here is both fragmentation and dissipation of selfhood (as Larkin says in "The Old Fools": "At death, you break up: the bits that were you / Start speeding apart from each other for ever") and movement towards this limit, this ultimate concentration of natural force.

The second "immortal diamond" seems at first sight to function as a metaphor for the resurrected body, imagined as immaculate and filled with light; but the first "immortal diamond" gets in the way of this metaphorization. The poem is not saying that "poor potsherds" (e.g. human cadavers) are, metaphorically speaking, really "immortal diamond" thanks to the intervening miracle of divine grace, but that there is a fundamental identity between the limit-point of natural process and the glittering prize of redemption. In an important sense, the second "immortal diamond" is *not* a metaphor: the tautological statement "immortal diamond / Is immortal diamond" says rather that at the true limit the temporal and the eternal fuse and are literally the same.

"That Nature is a Heraclitean Fire" redresses the Terrible Sonnets' sense of being immured within a self and a history beyond salvation by pursuing a radically different understanding of self and history. In this understanding, salvation is no longer the intervention of an absolute exception redeeming the sordidness of nature, but rather the gathering and consummation of a transformative, self-shattering power that is the cosmic Christ "eternally present in time as in nature". What succeeds the cold world of solitary perdition is for Hopkins a world of fire, of continuously raging trans-human energy.

The Aesthetics of Dejection

In the June of 1797 some long-expected friends paid a visit to the author's cottage; and on the morning of their arrival, he met with an accident, which disabled him from walking during the whole time of their stay. One evening, when they had left him for a few hours, he composed the following lines in the garden-bower.

S. T. Coleridge, *This Lime-Tree Bower My Prison*

Positioning himself ironically in relation to the Romantics, Philip Larkin famously said that deprivation was to him what daffodils were to Wordsworth. It is tempting to say that what deprivation was to Larkin, incapacitation was to Coleridge: so many of his great poems are concerned with being laid low, immobilised or disabled, as their author was in various ways throughout much of his creative life. "Dejection" is the name Coleridge gave to the most severe incapacitation of which he himself as a poet was capable: a failure of imaginative power. The "inanimate cold world" of his poem "Dejection: An Ode" is a world in which this power, "my shaping spirit of imagination", has ceased to be effective: a waste land in which the forms of the world stand bare.

In "This Lime-Tree Bower My Prison", imagination is a means of consolation, able to repair or at least mitigate the discomforts of isolation. The poem closes with the hope that while Coleridge and his friends (Charles and Mary Lamb) are parted, they may nevertheless separately "lift the soul, and contemplate / With lively joy the joys we cannot share", and in doing so partake of a universal spirit that includes them all:

My gentle-hearted Charles! When the last rook
Beat its straight path along the dusky air
Homewards, I blest it! deeming its black wing
(Now a dim speck, now vanishing in light)
Had cross'd the mighty Orb's dilated glory,
While thou stood'st gazing; or, when all was still,
Flew creeking o'er thy head, and had a charm
For thee, my gentle-hearted Charles, to whom
No sound is dissonant which tells of Life.

"Life" here is a universal consonance, the conviviality of all living things; and its ruling metaphor is the light of the "mighty Orb", which governs the appearance and disappearance of all that lives. The rook's "black wing" vanishes (from one point of view) into the haze of sunset and reappears (from another) in passing relief against the sun's "dilated glory". Coleridge and Lamb are creatures under the same sun, and the impulse of the one to bless is felicitously joined to the other's susceptibility to "charm", that cordial receptivity on account of which Coleridge three times calls him "gentle-hearted".

This passage involves a double referential movement, typical of Coleridge's devout Romanticism, from the particular to the universal and back again. The rook's dissonant "creeking" is made consonant with all other natural sounds by being referred to the universal "Life" of which it "tells". At the same time, it is in the particular heart of Coleridge's "gentle-hearted Charles" that this consonance is felt and realised. The spiritual impulse that rises up in a blessing meant for all creation finds its mark in a particular beloved person. In a similar fashion, in "The Rime of the Ancient Mariner" the poem's appeal to an all-encompassing love of "[b]oth man and bird and beast" is tied to the particular pragmatics of the Mariner's address to the

Wedding Guest, who must moreover be separated from the ceremonial throng of the wedding celebrations in order to hear it.

What is the relationship between this particular structure of address and the universal love that is its theme? The middle term that it bypasses is that of ordinary sociality: being with other people rather than in seclusion from them. The theme of universal love cannot be announced directly to the crowd, but must be addressed to an individual soul distracted by charm or enchantment from the distractions of the social whirl. This is why it is contrived that the Ancient Mariner should be left as the sole survivor of his vessel's crew, and thereby freed to confront nature as pure protean multiplicity: "The many men, so beautiful! / And they all dead did lie: / And a thousand thousand slimy things / Lived on; and so did I". We may grasp here the stricture that links the most generous spiritual capacity to the most drastic social privation, the most all-encompassing natural vision to the most restricted personal circumstances.

The well-known story of the "person on business from Porlock" who interrupted the composition of "Kubla Khan" is inseparably annexed to the poem itself, so that the poem's alleged incompletion seems less like an accident, a worldly contingency striking the text from outside and cutting it off abruptly, than an intrinsic aspect of the narrative to which it belongs. It is possible to read "Kubla Khan", together with Coleridge's note presenting the poem and explaining the circumstances of its composition, as a single text, the title of which might be ""Kubla Khan"": a fable about the relationship between the spheres of "business" and "tranquility", *otium* and *negotium*, and at the same time the story of a lost vision and a whole reduced to a fragment.

The "stately pleasure dome" of the poem, an immense walled garden, is like the garden-bower of "This Lime-Tree

Bower My Prison" an enclosure, a place of retreat and isolation from the business of the world. While "Kubla Khan" the poem presents the refuge as a place of demonic enchantment, whose recreation in verse has the power to bewitch the outside world, the story of ""Kubla Khan"" is one in which the outside world intervenes to break the spell of private self-absorption, leaving a part-poem that can only gesture towards the unbroken splendour of the total vision of which it is a fragment.

In addition to "Kubla Khan", the poem, and ""Kubla Khan"" the story of the poem, there is a third, phantom text: the lost original, the *ur*-"Kubla Khan" effaced by the arrival of the person from Porlock. But the visitor's intrusion is not the first mishap in the story Coleridge tells of the *ur*-"Kubla Khan"'s composition in reverie, but rather one in a series of narrative jolts and displacements:

> In the summer of the year 1797, the Author, then in ill health, had retired to a lonely farm-house between Porlock and Linton, on the Exmoor confines of Somerset and Devonshire. In consequence of a slight indisposition, an anodyne had been prescribed, from the effects of which he fell asleep in his chair at the moment that he was reading the following sentence, or words of the same substance, in "Purchas's Pilgrimage": "Here the Khan Kubla commanded a palace to be built, and a stately garden thereunto. And thus ten miles of fertile ground were inclosed with a wall".

The first displacement is quite literal: the poet is removed from society, retiring to secluded spot in a region between places, on the "Exmoor confines" between Porlock and Linton, Somerset and Devonshire. The "person on business from Porlock" is a person from town, visiting the wild, liminal place to which Coleridge had "retired" in order to take himself away from the world's business. The poet is not altogether himself; a "slight indisposition" has lead to the prescription of an "anodyne" (presumably laudanum), which robs him of his concentration in the middle of reading a passage in "Purchas's Pilgrimage" (a narrative about travel, both geographical and spiritual), causing him to fall asleep in his chair. Coleridge quotes the passage, but approximately, giving "words of the same substance" in place of the original text (which amongst other things refers to "a *sumptuous* house of pleasure" – compare Coleridge's "sunny" and "stately").

By this sequence of trips, translocations and substitutions we are conveyed to the state of reverie in which the ur-"Kubla Khan" manifests itself:

> The Author continued for about three hours in a profound sleep, at least of the external senses, during which time he has the most vivid confidence, that he could not have composed less than from two to three hundred lines; if that indeed can be called composition in which all the images rose up before him as *things*, with a parallel production of the correspondent expressions, without any sensation or consciousness of effort.

This "profound" sleep is both profound and superficial, as the qualifying phrase "at least of the external senses" suggests: the external world is put far away, and along with it any "sensation or consciousness of effort" in mental activity, and yet a sequence of lucid manifestations is able to occur in which both images and "correspondent expressions" are produced, the former rising up "as *things*" before the slumbering poet. We may take it that images do not present themselves before "the external senses" as *things*,

31

and that this inner ideation is thus not simply a replica or simulacrum of ordinary sensory experience. It is as *image itself*, the image-thing *in itself*, rather than the sensuous registration of its properties, that each image is presented.

Each image-thing is correlated with the expressive figure that will reproduce it, such that it is already a "poetic" image, the object or target of some figure of speech. In his reverie, Coleridge experiences the ur-"Kubla Khan" as the correlation of a series of linguistic tropes with a series of corresponding acts of cognition; except that in his account the conventional causality running from trope to image (that is, from reading to ideation, seeing in the mind's eye) is suspended: each image simply occurs "without any sensation or consciousness of effort" as a pure cognitive event, fortuitously shadowed by the "parallel production" of its figurative correlate.

In this passage, a "vivid confidence" (entertained in the present tense: the author's confidence remains vivid, even if the experience in which it confides has been lost) contends with an equivocation over the sense of "composition". Coleridge is confident that he composed not less than "two to three hundred lines" of verse, but the experience of presiding, in one's sleep, over a succession of poetic images and "correspondent expressions" would not seem to lend itself to quantification of this kind. While the verses of "Kubla Khan" do present a series of images felicitously expressed, they also involve devices of another order, for example the simile that describes the "swift half-intermitted burst" of the fountain from the cavern into which the Aleph flows as being "momently...forced" as if "the earth in fast thick pants were breathing". While the matter of the poem may have arisen spontaneously, its organization and resulting contexture are evidently the outcome of an active labour of arrangement.

The narrative of ""Kubla Khan"" now moves forwards into its most famous episode, the visit of the person from Porlock:

> On awaking he appeared to himself to have a distinct recollection of the whole, and taking his pen, ink and paper, instantly and eagerly wrote down the lines that are here preserved. At this moment he was unfortunately called out by a person on business from Porlock, and detained by him above an hour, and on his return to his room, found, to his no small surprise and mortification, that though he still retained some vague and dim recollection of the general purport of the vision, yet, with the exception of some eight or ten scattered lines and images, all the rest had passed away like the images on the surface of a stream into which a stone has been cast, but, alas! without the after restoration of the latter!

The replacement of a "distinct recollection of the whole" with "some vague and dim recollection of the general purport of the vision" echoes Coleridge's replacement of the literal text of the passage from "Purchas's Pilgrimage" with "words of the same substance", and the transmutation of that "substance" into the dream vision of the ur-"Kubla Khan". Such transmutation is the means by which the vision is both conjured and lost, as the "substance" or "general purport" which passes from "Purchas's Pilgrimage" into the dream vision, and from the dream vision into the "vague and dim recollection" which sustains the waking poet's "vivid confidence" in the reality of that which he has lost.

Something of the weirdness of Coleridge's conception of the poetic imagination comes into focus here. ""Kubla Khan"" is such a consistently, almost leg-pullingly, implausible account, like a ghost story or shaggy-dog tale, that one can readily believe that it was simply invented by Coleridge after the fact, as a fanciful and intriguing apology for a poem that had started well but that he had found himself unable to finish. Even the notion that "Kubla Khan" is *un*-finished is questionable: its closing cadences certainly give the impression of a poem that has run its course.

The folk-retelling of ""Kubla Khan"" boils down to: poet enters supernatural / drug-induced reverie, has dream vision, awakes, is interrupted by busybody, and after busybody has departed can remember only a fragment of the vision. Moral: busybodies are bad for visionary poetry. But this version tellingly gets a part of the story wrong: the written part of "Kubla Khan" is not the little that Coleridge could remember *after* the person from Porlock had left, but the "instantly and eagerly" transcribed substance of the *ur*-"Kubla Khan", accurately recorded right up until the moment of interruption. ""Kubla Khan"" effectively claims of "Kubla Kan", not that it is the result of the poet's clutching at the straws of his fleeting recollections of the vision, but that it is *exactly* what was composed in the reverie – up to a point.

In this way, ""Kubla Khan"" manages to be a story about both plenitude and loss. It frames the poem "Kubla Khan" as an impossible artefact, a fragment recovered from a realm of cognition where images are things and things are directly and effortlessly correlated with figures of speech, while at the same time emphasising the inaccessibility of this realm from the domain of normal consciousness, the waking mind of the man of the world who has been talking business with a visitor. The otherworldly and the worldly are placed in opposition, and correlated with a series of other oppositions: tranquillity and business, possession and dispossession, clarity and confusion, unity and dispersal. It is within this scheme of oppositions that the "cold world" of the

"Dejection" ode takes its place.

One of the greatest of Coleridge's poems, "Dejection: An Ode" is also one of the most bitterly circumstanced, written during a period of ill-health, agonizing discomfort, financial worry and deepening domestic discord. A poem of "dull pain", of "grief without a pang, void, dark, and drear, / A stifled, drowsy, unimpassion'd grief", it is however as much concerned with the condition of being unable to feel and express an affliction as it is with the affliction itself.

Let us begin with the fourth section, which says almost everything:

> O Lady! We receive but what we give,
> And in our life alone does Nature live:
> Ours is her wedding-garment, ours her shroud!
> And would we aught behold, of higher worth,
> Than that inanimate cold world allow'd
> To the poor loveless ever-anxious crowd,
> Ah! From the soul itself must issue forth
> A light, a glory, a fair luminous cloud
> Enveloping the Earth –
> And from the soul itself must there be sent
> A sweet and potent voice, of its own birth,
> Of all sweet sounds the life and element.

Three questions arise here. Firstly, there is the question of life and of the proper: of the priority of what is "ours", what belongs to "our life" and issues from "the soul itself". Secondly, there is the relationship between the "glory" that is properly ours and the natural world which it enfolds and invests. Thirdly, there is the status of the enveloped earth itself, the "inanimate cold world" which reveals itself as such to "the poor loveless ever-anxious crowd" of the unpropertied.

On the first point, it is a matter of identifying the origin of what "[w]e receive" from "Nature", and of that part of what "we...behold" which corresponds to our own desire for things "of higher worth". Receiving, and beholding that which one would "aught behold", are different modes of apprehension to merely being "allow'd" a glimpse of something. To receive a thing is to make it one's own, to translate it into one's own frame of reference (as when we speak, for example, of the "critical reception" of a work of art). The things that we apprehend in this way already have a relationship to our own desires: they are objects of our choosing, love-objects. Coleridge's claim, therefore, that "we receive but what we give", does not mean that "Nature" is a mirage solipsistically conjured by the soul out of thin air, but that our joy in nature is a joy fostered by our own powers of sympathetic attention.

On the second point, the relationship between the "glory" emanating from the soul and the bare "Earth" itself is one of enclosure, a symbolic enfolding (or costuming: "ours is her wedding-garment, ours her shroud") that simultaneously illuminates and obscures ("a fair luminous cloud"). This enfolding is an appropriation, a making-proper: life is properly the life of the living, and nature comes to life through becoming property, like a bride given in marriage. At the same time, the soul animates nature through the sending of its "sweet and potent voice...[o]f all sweet sounds the life and element". Insofar as nature speaks, or sings, it is the soul that is speaking or singing: it is our life alone that lives in nature. The soul's potency thus returns to itself in a circuit of appropriation, giving life to itself through its ability to animate natural objects, to invest them with symbolic significance. Nature serves as the conduit for desire, which returns to itself in language and as property.

On the third point, it is clear that neither "life" nor

"worth" nor "light" inheres in the natural world itself, which shows itself as "inanimate" and "cold" to those whom poverty, anxiety and exhaustion have robbed of their spiritual assets, their capacity for sympathetic attention. Again, the claim here is not that nature does not exist apart from our perceptions of it, but on the contrary that nature has a way of existing that is completely indifferent to our aesthetic and moral values: that far from being the teeming matrix of "life itself" out of which individual souls are formed (and arrive "trailing clouds of glory") nature is intrinsically lifeless and inglorious, affording nothing "of higher worth" on its own account.

The "poor loveless ever-anxious crowd" that must live, so to speak, on the meager allowance afforded by the "inanimate cold world" is a politically resonant figure of the multitude: a spiritually impoverished mass, sunk into Wordsworth's "savage torpor", that represents the unbinding of polity and the dispersal of a bare human animality without regard for life or property. The distinction of the poet – his *elevation* – is precisely a distinction from this unhappy multitude: "dejection" is, ultimately, the state of being lowered to their condition.

It is not for nothing that Wordsworth's response to the "Dejection" ode, the poem "Resolution and Independence", centres on the lone "leech gatherer" as a figure of generic humanity, demonstrating that the poet realises and concentrates a universal power of mental fortitude that even the most reduced circumstances cannot eliminate. But the leech gather is again a solitary figure, set apart from the crowd: the indomitable resolution he represents is an alchemically reduced, spiritualised form of that inalienable property so threatened by the alienated mob.

The "inanimate cold world" of the "Dejection" ode triangulates social withdrawal, emotional torpor and spiritual devastation, without the poem's being able to name any of these things as its primary cause. In a similar fashion, Larkin's "Love again" is unable, finally, to say where the bitterness and jealous rage of its opening lines originates. "Something to do with violence, / A long way back", Larkin suggests; but this violence, recapitulated in the poem's own curt obscenities, is simply posited without apparent cause or motive, and operates structurally, as a distant trauma, without itself becoming a cause or motive in turn. To have "[s]omething to do with" violence is to be bound up with it, contingently associated with it, without necessarily being caused by it; especially when it is placed "a long way back", out of the range of immediate causal influence.

We might say that, like Coleridge, the speaker of "Love again" "met with an accident, which disabled him", and this disablement is figured in the poem as both an inability to know what to do ("the drink gone dead, without showing how / To meet tomorrow, and afterwards") and an inability to *not* know what is happening ("[a]nd me supposed to be ignorant, / Or find it funny, or not to care", but clearly unable to do any of these things). Those for whom love *works*, for whom it is not the arid repetition of violence ("wanking at ten-past three"), are somehow able to overcome both of these impasses, being overtaken by a force that "sways them on in a sort of sense" without requiring them, as Larkin requires himself, to make sense of it in return. But "this element / Which spreads through other lives like a tree" is no more explicable than Larkin's "violence", and may indeed ultimately be the same thing.

Coleridge's amorous obsession with Sara Hutchinson, to whom an earlier version of the "Dejection" ode was addressed as a letter, was characterised, as such obsessions usually are, by a similar cognitive immobilization. But the immobilization may in fact have been the point: the principal emotion conveyed by the "Letter to Sara Hutchinson" is a dread of action, coupled with a self-stupefying remorse at ever having had – again, in Larkin's words – "the blind persistence / To upset an existence / Just for one's own sake". If "persistence" is, conventionally and like love itself, "blind", then it may be that abstinence, interruption, self-restraint are among the conditions of insight. In other words, it is not knowing that makes one unable to act, but failing to act that makes one able to know.

William Blake's lucid proverbs, "if the fool would persist in his folly, he would become wise", and, "the road of excess leads to the palace of wisdom", are meant to lead one to a wisdom distinct from knowledge, a wisdom that can only be reached through blind and excessive persistence. The goal of such persistence is the full realization of one's own nature: for "the fool" to persist in "his folly" is for him to elaborate his innate foolishness to the highest degree. For Wordsworth, it is "Nature" that accomplishes this realization through the persistent moulding of human sensibility, not by exposing itself to human knowledge but by exposing the knowing mind to itself as the seat of its own natural powers. The path taken by Coleridge in "Dejection: An Ode" is, by contrast, one of intellectual self-dissection, with the explicit goal of diverting or overcoming the pressure of painful emotion:

> For not to speak of what I needs must feel,
> But to be still and patient, all I can;
> And haply by abstruse research to steal
> From my own nature all the natural Man –
> This was my sole resource, my only plan:
> Till that which suits a part infects the whole,
> And now is almost grown the habit of my Soul.

"[W]hat I needs *must*" and "all I *can*" are here counterposed as separate and contending powers: one the one hand, a force of "feeling", emanating from "the natural Man", which impels one to speak, and on the other a capacity for stillness fortified by "abstruse research". Considered in the light of Wordsworth's famous dicta concerning poetry – "the spontaneous overflow of powerful feeling", "emotion recollected in tranquility", and so forth – this deliberate stifling of emotive speech, this patient exercise of self-thwarting intellectual cunning, appears as a "plan" of singular perversity.

The final couplet of the lines quoted above plays on the double sense of "habit" as both covering garment and mental custom. Just as "that which suits" (e.g. clothes and covers) "a part" can by extension become a "habit" covering the entire body, so the entirety of one's inner life can come to be taken over by the mental customs one has cultivated in order to deal with one intolerable portion of it. In the biblical story of the Garden of Eden, the immediate consequence of Adam and Eve's eating the fruit of the tree of the knowledge of good and evil is that they know that they are naked, and try to cover their sexual organs. After the fall, the body infected by sexual shame becomes the sinful flesh, corrupt in its entirety: the sexual "part" disorganises the body's integrity. The separation in this passage between the pressure of "what I needs must feel" and the intellectual imperatives of patient self-knowledge and self-control is the result of a struggle to regain this compromised integrity, to rid "my own nature" of "the natural *Man*": the "old Adam", the sexed being whose nature is never wholly his own.

In a sense, the question here is whether the Wordsworthian "egotistical sublime" can manage the discovery within itself of a sexual "part", or whether the universal spirit hymned in Coleridge's poetry can accommodate the inexorable partiality of erotic interest. All-encompassing love of humanity is one thing; the irruption of inappropriate sexual feeling, with all its consequent anxieties and entanglements, quite another. It is again a matter of sociality, of *others* – this time in the guise of potential objects (and subjects) of desire, "other lives" through which desire "spreads...like a tree". According to Coleridge, the function of the "esemplastic" power of imaginative genius is to render the forms of the world commensurable with one another, bringing them together into a higher unity (of word and image, image and thing, as in the dream vision of ""Kubla Khan""). The haphazardness of sexual affinity, in which one being is attracted to another on the basis of the irremediable particularity of each, both confounds the project of this "shaping spirit" and demonstrates how a world might nevertheless be woven out of myriad *local* truths borne of affinitive connections, amorous encounters.

Coleridge's cold world is, like Hopkins's, a world determined by the absence of a transcendent power, a vital principle that had sustained both the world itself and the poet's sympathetic connection with it. The extinction of this power leaves behind it a world of empty, incoherent manifestation, a world that continues to exist only by mistake. It also leaves the poet unable to accomplish a new connection with the world, except through self-mortification, an attempt to reconcile oneself with the destitution of reality by systematically undermining one's own ability to entertain illusions. Dejection is a condition of self-inflicted aesthetic privation, a willed crisis of language. And yet the conclusion of "Dejection: An Ode" affirms, finally, the validity of love and the truth borne by amorous affinity, separating Coleridge's admiration for Sara Hutchinson from his own tortured, miserable self-interest; marvelling, even, at the choice that something in him made to be connected with something beyond him:

> Joy lift her spirit, joy attune her voice;
> To her may all things live, from Pole to Pole,
> Their life the eddying of her living soul!
>   O simple spirit, guided from above,
> Dear Lady! Friend devoutest of my choice,
> Thus may'st thou ever, evermore rejoice.

A Sermon In The Name Of Death

Something must have happened to the militant, to separate him or her from the satisfactions of everyday life. Even in situations where the conditions of everyday life are not in the least satisfactory, where harsh suffering and gnawing anguish are the order of the day, the militant is a person set apart. We will not understand her if we suppose her to be purely a creature of anger and bitterness: what distinguishes her is not the intensity of her outrage, but the fact of her separation. She is someone who has decisively rejected every source of consolation: every hope that tomorrow will of its own accord come bearing some respite, some unanticipated good news.

The militant does not live in the same world as everyone else. Even the communist fighter who vigorously upholds the maxim that all are equal, who tirelessly hurls herself across the boundaries of class and communal identity in order to be in equality with others, affirms through these very transgressions her extrication from the world in which those others themselves live. Theirs is a world of inequalities, a world ineluctably structured by distinctions both gross and fine between persons: a world in which the firebrand with a passion for equality will always appear as a curious interloper, a person from *outside*.

Something must have happened, or have failed to happen. There may have been no single disaster, no totally devastating betrayal of trust in the world. The militant may even have the mildest of personal backgrounds: she is not infrequently in fact a child of privilege, of loving and educated parents who may have imagined that their offspring would be destined for a life of quiet professional accomplishment. Even the most charmed existence is not without its disappointments, but these are seldom sufficient in themselves to make the whole of life seem accursed. It is not merely a question of *overreacting*, of failing to understand the true scale of human misfortune and hence to recognise the relative triviality of one's own upsets. There is no common measure, whether just or inflated, that can connect the world of the militant with the world she has forsaken.

For the adolescent in revolt, a militant in prototype, the world is a model for two contradictory sets of axioms: the axioms of *life* and those of (a) *truth*. The problem this contradiction presents is not immediately personal in character, although personal problems inevitably figure in its elaboration. It has the appearance of a cosmic struggle, a battle for the soul of the world. Conventional wisdom tells us that this is self-aggrandisement, a consequence of taking one's inner turmoil too seriously and projecting one's private libidinal difficulties onto a metaphysical canvas. Adolescents have - or like to think they have - souls; the world has none. But this verdict presupposes that the outcome of the struggle is already decided: that life itself is all there is to life, and that there is no place at all in the "real" world for truth. The adolescent reopens the question; the militant pursues a solution.

What are the axioms of life? They are those which are verified by existing society, the society administered by one's parents and teachers and inhabited by one's peers and siblings. These are, firstly, that life *is unfair*: that existence is a struggle, at every level, between unequally matched forces; that there are winners and losers; that the prizes to be won are status and material wealth, and the forfeits deprivation and bitter humiliation. Secondly, that life *goes on*: that there is an everlasting continuity between life as it is now and, *mutatis mutandis*, life as it has always been; that life will at best ignore and at worst contemptuously obliterate any attempt to live otherwise than in the self-interested service of a limited set of goods. Life "goes on" because it is essentially homeostatic, a self-sustaining and self-correcting order. It is not building inexorably towards a moment of ultimate crisis when its contradictions will shake it to pieces. None of life's little disasters - or even its appalling, exorbitant horrors – has ever managed to put a stop to all of this. Maybe one day, an asteroid; but it won't come with a hammer and sickle painted on the side.

The axioms of life are those of a nihilism; they govern a life without values, without any end or purpose save its own continuation. This may seem counter-intuitive: isn't it the nihilist who fails to value life, to recognise the sanctity and dignity of living beings? What other values can there be besides those which flow from life itself, the values of the living? But this self-valuation of the living present encloses a void, a total absence of regard for anything besides itself; which is why the teenage daughter who accuses her mother – who never does anything that is not for the good of the family – of "selfishness" has a certain terrible justice on her side. Truly to value something is to value it "more than life itself", more than that which blindly survives in one's own life.

Accordingly, it is very clear why adolescent revolt so often involves of a turn towards the symbolism of death: such symbols mark the exits from the convivial homeostasis of existing society, and serve as portals to the land of the dead.

The video for Britney Spears's 2005 single "Everytime" depicts the troubled pop star at the end of her tether: hounded by paparazzi, rowing violently with a male partner, and eventually lying in a bath submerging her head beneath the milky bathwater. An angelic doppelganger-Britney then observes herself being pulled from the bath by the same partner and subjected to a failed resuscitation attempt in hospital, before passing along to the next room where a woman is cradling her newborn child. This juxtaposition of images of death and new life is apparently part of a fantasy sequence in the mind of the original Britney-in-the-bath, whom we finally see lifting her head back out of the water with a reassuring smile: she has chosen to live after all.

The officially released video presents a somewhat toned-down version of a concept that originally played much more explicitly with the theme of suicide, hinting strongly at an overdose. Following criticism of the original video from various quarters, Britney's label felt compelled to issue a statement clarifying that the singer did not "endorse [suicide] as a *solution* to any individual". The wording is significant: a famous US court case of the 1980s was brought against the heavy metal singer Ozzy Osbourne by the parents of John McCollum, a teenager who had killed himself with a shotgun allegedly whilst listening to Osbourne's "Suicide Solution".

The lyrics of "Suicide Solution" are in fact concerned with alcohol addiction, and were written by Osbourne's bandmate Bob Daisley, in the aftermath of AC/DC singer Bon Scott's alcohol-related death from hypothermia, with the intention of warning Ozzy that he too was dissolving his life in drink. Nevertheless, in court it was argued that the song not only endorsed suicide as a solution to life's problems, but also contained irresistibly persuasive subliminal messages urging the listener to "Get the gun and try it! Shoot, Shoot, Shoot". The case fed into an ongoing moral panic among US Christians about heavy metal's satanic influence; it is much the same constituency, one imagines, that needed to be reassured that the once-wholesome Britney Spears was not also peddling a deadly "suicide solution", a toxic reagent by which the souls of the nation's teenagers would be fatally corroded.

Even in its bowdlerised form, the "Everytime" video presents a moment of existential indecision, a fugue of suicidal ideation in which the singer fantasises about her own death. A fan-generated clip on the video-sharing website YouTube pairs these images with the music of Xasthur, a one-man "black metal" band from Alhambra, California. In the clip, Britney's head disappears beneath the surface of the bathwater to the accompaniment of a churning miasma of distorted minor arpeggios, mechanically pounding drums, off-key synths and distant, howling vocals. This appalling sonic aura, the pairing implies, is the true sound of Britney's inner emotional chaos. The music thus restores the lost "suicidal" content to the video, sound-tracking its implicit narrative. The clip nominates the voided, unearthly screams of Malefic (the pseudonym of Scott Conner, Xasthur's creator) as the phantom complement of Britney's saccharine, roboticised vocals.

Suicide is a recurring theme in Xasthur's music; but it is suicide viewed not as a "solution", a resolution of life's problems, but as capitulation, the obedient response to a deadly interpellation. The dissonant sound-world of Malefic's compositions is designed to confront the listener with the waste and horror of human existence, the worth-lessness of all human striving: the affect it aims to induce is one of overwhelming despair. The listener who endures this "arcane and misanthropic projection" of unsparing negativity and is not moved to self-harm will thereby have demonstrated a certain resilience, albeit the resilience of self-delusion. For in spite of the opposition of authentic inner "strength" to corrupt, worldly "weakness" that often charac-terises depressive black metal artists' statements of intent, it is not inner resolve that protects the listener from despair but a failure of rational consistency. The purpose of

Xasthur's music is to hold up a musical mirror to the world, revealing life as a hopeless situation in which suicide is the only *logical* course of action.

It is a distorting mirror, and the suicidal logic of the world it reflects is a distorted logic: that of depressive thinking, a supremely logical mode of thought. Depressive thinking is driven not by affect but by its own detached automatism. It is neither a reflection on, nor an obsession with, the thinker's own sadness, which is on the contrary invisible to it (the realization that one is in fact grief-stricken or unbearably sad is often the first emotional touchstone of a person emerging from depression). At its centre is a simple identification: life and death are identical, the axioms of life are axioms of death. There is no *difference* between being alive and being dead, except that the living suffer.

Depressive thinking is simultaneously intensely lucid and intensely blinkered: ruthlessly and brilliantly reductive, it is able to demolish any consoling counter-argument by referring it immediately to the ground zero of its own originary devastation. It is monotonous in the same way that Xasthur's music is monotonous, endlessly circling around the same motifs. The world it composes is one in which the light of the world has gone out, and every being formerly illuminated by that light now stands with every other in a common obscurity. The cover of Xasthur's *Defective Epitaph* accordingly depicts an array of tombstones, each inscribed with an identical barcode (for the number zero): an image of the land of the dead, in which living itself appears as an absurd and insupportable excrescence.

If Xasthur's music shows us what is in the mirror of depression – our own distorted figures, minimally distinguished from the abyss that surrounds and will soon engulf them – it also however shows us the mirror itself, thereby enabling us to see what depressive thinking itself consistently screens out: the facticity of its own logic, of the banally compulsive ideation that supports the consistency of its twilight world. By giving form to this compulsion, it both attracts its listeners to it, drawing them into its ambit, and estranges them from it, enabling them to place it at a distance. Xasthur's image of despair is even a little bit silly: the photograph of Malefic's home studio that appears on the inner sleeve of *Defective Epitaph* shows two B. C. Rich guitars propped up by the far wall, their stylised devil-horned bodies a reminder of the cartoonish pomp with which heavy metal has traditionally paid its respects to the powers of darkness. Even the bar-coded tombstones on the cover are bleakly funny in their own way.

While Xasthur's music may be conceived as a kind of psychic assault, an attempt to disorientate and demoralise the listener, it is also strangely tranquil, almost comforting, in its sonic texture. The blast-beats on the drums are muted so that what would have been a pummelling assault up-close becomes part of the throb and churn of the guitar arrangements, which in turn are based around ringing arpeggios and chord progressions or single-note lines sustained through rapid "tremolo" picking. The effect of the latter is to mask the distinction between attack, sustain and decay in the articulation of each note or chord: the sound is closer to that of a bowed instrument played tremolo-style. In general, then, the percussive elements of the music are subordinated to texture, to the creation of a continuous yet palpitating tone.

Xasthur's musical antecedents here are the Norwegian black metal bands of the early 1990s, such as Burzum and Darkthrone, whose combination of speed-picked guitar lines and frenetic blast-beat drumming evoked the furious urgency of the "wild flight" of the Norse Oskari, horsemen of the sky. The hypnotic aspects of this style are coupled with the thrill of the chase, of being swept up insensibly into a wild and violent multitude: the intensity of the sound is a *hectic* intensity, an intensity of movement. With Xasthur, the same musical elements and techniques are dedicated to the establishment of a static, immobilised sound-image, a downwards spiral: the hypnotic aspect of the original sound is foregrounded, while the adrenaline-driven rage of early black metal is channelled into cryptic, tormented howling.

Warlike and insurrectionary, the Norwegian bands who declared that "black metal *ist Krieg*" sought to rouse their followers from what they saw as the apathy of a Christianised, egalitarian society, recalling them to the natural aristocracy of their pagan national roots. Some manifestations of this ideology were more overtly fascist than others; and some, such as that propounded by Burzum's Varg Vikernes, were so *ultra*-fascist that even those attracted by the politics of the extreme right wing were apt to be alienated by the concerted loathing of humanity they evinced. But the political attitudes of the progenitors of black metal were generally expressions of a drive to develop an ideology maximally incompatible with the peaceful social democratic self-image of Norwegian society: they were less about allegiance to nationalist causes than they were about generating antagonism.

The original Norwegian black metal scene was a brief explosion of anti-social outrage, marked by an escalation of criminality (from graveyard desecration to church-burning and murder) and terminated by internecine conflict (the infamous killing of Mayhem's Euronymous by Varg Vikernes). Much of the subsequent history of the genre has been characterised by a morbid reverence for the mythologised time in which these original events unfolded, a fascination with its malevolent *dramatis personae* and their horrifying excesses. It is thus possible to speak of a "late", or "belated", black metal, a music in which the fantasy of a violently anti-heroic "dream-time" plays a significant role. The shift, in Xasthur and other "late" black metal bands, from warlike belligerence to depressive introspection may be understood as a reaction to precisely this belatedness.

It is significant that a common term of approbation in black metal circles is "true" (as in "true Norwegian black metal"). The early years of the genre were stimulated by a vigorous tape-trading scene, in which third- or fourth-generation copies of already low-quality recordings were circulated between devotees. Darkthrone's seminal "Transylvanian Hunger" was recorded with such a raw, hissy, compressed sound that a first-generation copy might easily have been mistaken for a live performance captured by a fan waving a Dictaphone. This cadaverous "necro" sound, degraded and degenerate, was originally an artefact of the limited means of production and distribution available to black metal musicians (Varg Vikernes's recordings as Burzum were largely funded by his mother). Almost from the beginning, however, it was established as a token of authenticity, a sign that the artist had sincerely broken away from what was regarded as a sterile and commercialised mainstream metal scene. Accordingly, low (or deliberately lowered) production values and primitive (by contemporary standards) recording techniques are one of the ways in which a black metal artist can demonstrate fidelity to the genre's roots.

"Late" black metal artists such as Xasthur and Striborg takes this sonic degradation a step further, emphasising the dissonant, eerie elements within the original template. Striborg's Sin Nanna reduces the guttural vocal rasp of black metal vocals from a menacing growl to a squawking death-rattle, the sound of some gnarled woodland spirit expectorating apoplectically in the darkness, while unmartialing the taut rumble of Darkthrone's blast beats into a chaotic clatter of freeform drumming. The aura the music diffuses is one of confused, asphyxiating dread, like an attack of sleep paralysis (or the experience, common among those who believe they have been abducted by supernatural beings, of waking in the darkness and finding oneself immobilized and invaded by a hostile presence). Xasthur, meanwhile, builds on the atonal riffing of Burzum and the disfigured counterpoint of Manes and Mütiilation to construct a sound-world in which consonance is continually menaced by intrusions from another harmonic universe. Guitars and synths are deliberately detuned so that complex multi-tracked arrangements curdle and pulse with malign energy. If the hypnotic, tranquilising texture of the music suggests a return to the womb, the "disharmonic convergence" of Xasthur's compositional approach evokes a fouled and toxic antenatal environment.

The introversion (literally, "turning inwards") of late black metal must be understood as a development of the genre's original combative, anti-social stance. Malefic's withering scorn for Californian metal scenesters is extended, in Xasthur's "Defective Epitaph", to the Californian ideology of New Age-y social progressiveness in general. The track titles include spiteful inversions and negations of New Age nostrums: "Legacy of human irrelevance", "Worship (the war against) Yourself", "Unblessed be". But to wage war on oneself, and especially to *worship* the forces which war within and against the self, is to uphold an ethic of inner conflict and self-overcoming (*not* self-realisation) which is by no means simply nihilistic. What is more, this ethic not only mirrors but intensifies the early Norwegian black metallers' ferocious attack on what they saw as the complacent mediocrity of a society dominated by liberal Judeo-Christian moral values.

For the sect who gathered around Euronymous's retail

outlet *Helvete,* anointing themselves black metal's "inner circle" and scheming to bring down their society by snarling at it, the temptation was always to regard themselves as an elect few, as superior beings dedicated to a true individualism in defiance of universal social conformity. Metal has always been anti-conformist, but it is also by and large anti-sectarian: a broad church, welcoming all persuasions. That is precisely why black metal had to separate itself from "commercial" metal, turning to a fundamentalist misprision of the satanic and megalomaniac tropes of the genre to legitimate its rejection of all those "posers" who betrayed their lack of sincerity by compromising with the established moral order. Unfortunately even Venom and Bathory, among the most artistically compelling of black metal's influences, were in reality less than wholly serious in their dedication to outrage and insurrection. Ultimately the only way to validate the "true" black metal was to make the transition from aesthetic iconoclasm to active criminal violence – from performing menacing stage acts with impaled pigs' heads and upside-down crosses to burning churches and ruthlessly murdering one's rivals.

In making this transition, black metal rapidly exhausted its capacity for real mayhem: the police cracked down, the most careless offenders received lengthy jail sentences, and most of the musicians reverted to corpse-painted theatrics: sociopathic individualism became once again a *spiritual* position. "Late" black metal is thus the inheritor of a re-aestheticising of a radically anti-aesthetic moment, a moment when the criterion for judging the validity of a piece of music was no longer its sensuous qualities or its cultural significance but rather the extent to which its creators' declarations of intent coincided with real acts of rebellion and destruction. As Ulrike Meinhof had said, in quite another context: other left-wing groups had merely theorised about revolutionary action; the RAF had actually gone out and *done* it. One should not overlook the role of the media in establishing this correlation between proclamation and deed, phantasmatically converting the former into the latter until *Greven* ("Count Grishnakh", a pseudonym of Varg Vikernes's) became precisely the figure of supernatural evil his creator had always wanted him to be. (Indeed, this is true of the RAF as well).

While Xasthur's music inhabits the re-spiritualised, re-aestheticised terrain of belated black metal, and in no way seeks to re-ignite the paroxysm of violence that shook Norwegian society in the early 1990s, it also radicalises the misanthropy of early black metal, annulling the sectarian elitism of the "inner circle" by pronouncing a judgement of irrelevance on all human endeavour. Here we must ask: is a consistent and thorough-going hatred of *all* humanity possible? Indifference towards humanity is not difficult to imagine: pretty much all of the universe is full of it pretty much all of the time. But *hatred* of humanity as such, of "the human precisely as human", is much more difficult to carry off.

Hatred is a human emotion; this means both that it is a general propensity of human beings and that it manifests itself distinctly in specific human individuals or collectivities, and is thus inexorably situated and partial. That is the first problem: the affect of hatred must always be borne by some human being. It cannot therefore be consistently both a) contempt for that which is inferior to oneself, and b) universal in scope, since a human being, included in its own hatred of all things human, cannot be inferior to itself.

The misanthropist must choose between two paths. The first is to make an exception for some special class of human being, and to include oneself in the exception. A few human beings are strong, pure, decent and worthy of survival. Even though the very essence of humanity is accursed, it is possible to live an aesthetically pleasing life. The conditions of such a life will include isolation from the "great masses" of humanity (concentrated as they are in the cities), emotional coldness and repression, and devotion to an external rule that will give coherence and meaning to one's actions. Thus, *mutatis mutandis*, H. P. Lovecraft's approbation for "Puritan inhibitions" as "attempts to make of life a work of art - to fashion a pattern of beauty in the hog-wallow that is animal existence", and the post-apocalyptic rural paganism dreamed of by Varg Vikernes.

The first path alternates with the second, according to which all of humanity remains accursed but is hated *from the standpoint of the inhuman* - in the first instance, of the dead. "Pure Depressive Black Funeral Doom Metal" exponent Nortt describes his music thus:

> The elegies of Nortt tell about death and darkness viewed from the dying and from the dead. They reveal a bitter hate towards life and its divine maker. It is pure misanthropy and blasphemy – not self-pity! The darkened soil is praised as the godforsaken heaven – a heaven in hell. In order to unchain oneself from the despair of life, follow the path of death! At a funereal pace and with a sombre, chanting voice, Nortt summons the forces in the night.

"Pure misanthropy...not self-pity": in order to be pure, misanthropy must be purified of any attachment to the human self that would fall within its remit. The allegiance of the misanthropist without reserve is to a world of the dead that despises and rejects that of the living. Xasthur's "Telepathic with the Deceased" engages the same conceit: "Haters of life are telepathic with the deceased. / Fragments of failure, some said it was art, for it only bears a meaning when all life is torn apart". We might call this affect tele-antipathy: the "spooky action at a distance" of "the dying and...the dead". It is unsurprising that a recurring theme in Xasthur's lyrics and song titles is that of *projection*. Total misanthropy forces a split in the human self: a self-projection into the realm of the inhuman, which is indiscernible from a projection from that realm into the human world.

The cold world of black metal is a deliberate freezing of the world, fixing it within a terminal image, in order that its frost-bitten surface may be shattered by anonymous, inhuman forces rising from the depths of the self. It is a withdrawal of affect from the world, in order to experience "the eerie bliss and torture of solitude" and so discover the forces at war within oneself. These operations must be understood as spiritual exercises, as forms of emotional fasting intended to release the soul from its worldly attachments. Such exercises are purely narcissistic and self-salving if they do not also release the soul *for* new worldly commitments. The vertiginous dysphoria of Xasthur's sound-world is not yet the focused displeasure of the militant, but a simulacrum – a spiritualisation – of malcontent. It embodies a will that that which is should not be, but not a will that that which is should be otherwise.

The Brain of Ulrike Meinhof

Das Konzept Stadtguerrilla der Roten Armee Fraktion basiert nicht auf einer optimistischen Einschätzung der Situation in der Bundesrepublik und Westberlin.

The RAF's urban guerrilla concept is not based on an optimistic overview of the situation in the Federal Republic and West Berlin.

We do not presume to know the mind of Ulrike Meinhof, and what follows is not to be a séance.

It has been the fate of Meinhof's name to be yoked to that of Andreas Baader, and so to be invoked as a byword for revolutionary desperation. Everyone knows that "the Baader-Meinhof gang" committed a number of outrages: bombings, kidnappings, bank robberies; the occasional perforation of bystanders. It is also well known that Meinhof died in confinement, officially of suicide. The conditions of that confinement, and the torment of isolation she was made to endure, somewhat confuse the matter of whether her death was self-inflicted or brought about by the authorities.

After she died, the brain of Ulrike Meinhof was removed and preserved in formaldehyde, in order that it might be studied for abnormalities. It is imaginable that a long period of solitary confinement in the "dead wing" of a maximum-security prison might inflict some neurological attrition. But the question put to the brain of Ulrike Meinhof was rather this: what is it that causes a young woman journalist from a middle-class background to renounce the privileges society has afforded her, join an armed unit of self-styled "urban guerrillas", and commence to wage a ferocious war against the powers of the state? Nobody of sound mind could consider such an aberrant course of action; and the ultimate causes of unsoundness of mind are to be found, as everyone now knows, in the neurological substrate of consciousness. In due course it was revealed that the brain of Ulrike Meinhof had undergone a surgical operation to remove a tumour, prior to becoming the brain of a militant: perhaps that is sufficient to explain everything.

Perhaps. Here is what Ulrike Meinhof wrote in April 1968 regarding the difference between protest and resistance:

Protest ist, wenn ich sage, das und das paßt mir nicht. Widerstand ist, wenn ich dafür sorge, daß das, was mir nicht paßt, nicht länger geschieht.

Protest is when I say that something does not suit me. Resistance is when I make sure that that which does not suit me no longer occurs.

Here is a telling shift in sense: from the Spanish slogan of resistance, *no pásaran*, they shall not pass, to *das paßt mir nicht*: that does not suit me (it is a poor fit; the colours do not match). Resistance is not when I stand against the advance of an enemy, but when I oppose myself to the recurrence of a source of displeasure.

Meinhof's statement distinguishes between speech and action as possible responses to this displeasure, between the speech of protest, in which the nuisance is identified, and the act of resistance which targets the source of displeasure and aims to remove it. It is clear that acting is more effective than speaking, that it "makes sure" of an outcome that speech can only gesture towards. In merely announcing my displeasure, not only do I do nothing to mitigate it, but I also fail to affect it at its source, to prevent it from recurring.

This is true even if what displeases me is the activity of

another person, who might be persuaded to act otherwise by my speech, since it is not merely the fact of my being displeased that is at issue, but the power the other has of displeasing me. Resistance addresses itself to this power: it seeks to render impotent that which is capable of occurring time and time again, displeasing me repeatedly. It is thus not merely a matter of negotiating with the world of facts, addressing this or that (*das und das*) inconvenience, but of reshaping the world in its potentiality, removing its potential for harm. Only when the world is no longer able to displease me, when that which displeases me *nicht länger geschieht*, will the proper task of resistance have been accomplished.

Resistance is thus resistance to everything in the world that has the power of displeasing me, to a world of unpleasure: a world, to use a term Meinhof seems to have relished, of *Dreck*. It may even be directed towards that which I find pleasing, or at least not directly unpleasant, insofar as the same power gives rise to my pleasures as is responsible for my displeasure. Consider a well-known anecdote: at a PLO training camp in Jordan, Andreas Baader announces to his Palestinian hosts, who are astonished and outraged by the sight of his female comrades sunbathing naked on the roof of their hut, that sexual and political emancipation must arrive together: "fucking and shooting are the same thing!" The *same* thing. Make love as you would make war. Pleasure must be separated from the power that supports it; the act of pleasure must become an act of warfare against that power. Not only, as naïve sexual liberationists would have it, against the prohibition of pleasure and the imposition of unpleasure; but also against the prescribed, sanctioned, obligatory pleasures.

In "Instincts and their Vicissitudes" (*Triebe ünd Triebschicksen*, which might alternatively be translated as "Drives and their Destinies"), Freud identifies the *drives* as those stimuli which are not relieved by motor action. A tiny human animal is restless and unsettled, and kicks its feet and waves its arms about. This does it no good: it is still hungry. By contrast, the discomfort I feel on sitting down on a sharp object is not the manifestation of a drive, as it is immediately relieved by standing up. The hungry human animal cries out, declaring that something is occurring that does not suit it; the mother comes, and it is fed.

In the realm of the drives, the hierarchy of effectiveness of protest and resistance in relation to unpleasure is inverted. For the helpless infant resistance to hunger is futile, as motor action is powerless to remove the displeasure arising from its famishment. Instead, it must raise its voice in protest, in order to attract the attention of someone who can provide it with what it needs. It happens that the world, and especially the world of middle-class West German citizens in 1968, provides many opportunities for *cathexis*, the connection of a drive-stimulus with some object that has the power to relieve it, to draw off its energies and dissipate them elsewhere. To live well in the world it is necessary to be able to form such cathexes between the drives and worldly objects: to love, Freud says, and work.

The world of the "urban guerrilla" is a world in which such opportunities for cathexis are held at bay; where the governing principles of love and work are replaced by a single alternative principle: that of *combat*. One does not petition hopefully for what one needs; one violently expropriates, in order that one might have in abundance. One does not stand patiently outside the prison, begging for the release of those held within: one takes hostages, and bargains with their lives. Above all, one does not negotiate, but issues unilateral demands and manifestoes, statements of requirements intended to guide action.

Ulrike Meinhof devoted a long text, "The Concept of the

Urban Guerrilla", to this principle of combat and to the new reality that it creates around it. Knowledge, theory, critical reflection: all are immediately subordinated to struggle, *Kampf*, which has no need of intellect except insofar as the latter is able to sharpen its tactics and assist in the refinement of its strategy. After the time of action it may be necessary to reflect, to synthesise the concrete knowledge gained thereby into a new awareness. But the time of action, the *now* of the known situation and the struggle taking place therein, is fundamentally disjoint from the time of reflection, which discerns the limits of its knowledge and joins sites together.

The time of action is above all not the time of the counter-factual, of what might have been. A section of Meinhof's text entitled "Concrete answers to concrete questions" takes up the question of whether or not the raid to get Andreas Baader out of police custody would have been undertaken if it had been known that Linke, an elderly librarian, would be shot and injured in the process. This question, Meinhof asserts, "can only be answered with a 'no'". But it is in any case a stupid question:

> But the question of what might have been is equivocal – pacifist, platonic, moralizing, non-partisan. Whoever seriously considers the freeing of prisoners does not put questions of this kind (*stellt sie nicht*) but seeks the answers herself. By this, people want to know whether we are as brutalised as the Springer press makes out (*darstellt*), they are putting our catechism to the question. They are trying to circumvent the issue of revolutionary struggle by bringing revolutionary struggle and bourgeois morality together, which does not go.

Here as before it is a question of that which "does not go":

revolutionary force and bourgeois morality are ill-suited, irreconcilable. While the latter consists of suppositions, the putting (*Stellung*) of "platonic" questions and the making-out (*Darstellung*) of hypotheses, the former exits altogether the field of such representations through the personally committed pursuit of concrete outcomes. However, Meinhof also asserts that consideration of all possibilities and circumstances (*aller Möglichkeiten und Umstände*) had given no ground for belief that a civilian, a non-entity in the combat situation, could – and would - get in the way.

The fact of Linke's *actually* having interposed his body (in the process of making a dash for the exit) between the militants and their objective is thus doubly unthinkable. Firstly, it will never have appeared as an object of prior speculation: the militant does not *posit*, but acts. Such action is not subject to the hesitations imposed by bourgeois morality, which refuses the concrete knowledge arising from action in favour of fearful confabulation about its possible evil consequences. The revolutionary is not greatly concerned with evils that have yet to occur, being primarily engaged in combating those evils which have *already* occurred and whose recurrence, if they are not opposed, is guaranteed.

Secondly, it was in any case *not conceivable* that a Linke should so appear and happen to be wounded. While the moralist plays with imaginary consequences, the activist plans and strategises. But Linke and his body do not appear anywhere in the graph of circumstances plotted by the comrades. The shooting of Linke attests to an abnormal modality of occurrence: a happenstance apart from all conceivable *Möglichkeiten und Umstände*, a groundless contingency. One cannot even say whether it would happen again, if the raid were to be repeated; thus, in a certain sense, like the "anecdotal" evidence discounted by scientific procedure,

it *did not really happen*. The brute fact of its occurrence proves
nothing, forms a link in no repeatable sequence of events. It
is clear that, for Meinhof, the line of questioning which seeks
to attach a strategic, political significance to the shooting of
poor Linke is simply the retrospective form of the bourgeois
superstition that frets about possible evil consequences.

There is a gap of symbolization here, which bourgeois
morality will invariably construe as a failing of moral
awareness but which persists – and, indeed, can only be
recognised for what it is – even when the claims of that
morality are suspended. Neither bourgeois morality nor the
ethics of revolutionary violence can accept and symbolise on
their own terms the groundless contingency of what
happens. The pre-eminent demand of bourgeois morality is
for social peace, for the security of property. According to
this morality, the shooting of Linke is a symptom of "brutal-
ization", a dehumanised recklessness about human life
(conceived as the property of individuals, a property
vulnerable to loss or damage). It is immoral to endanger life
(qua property), and therefore immoral to engage in
hazardous and violent action, except for the ultimate
purpose of preserving or defending life (qua property).
Bourgeois morality is accordingly unable to conceptualise a
life-process in which hazard and insecurity play an intrinsic
part: hence its equation of safety with decency, and its
association of poverty, with all its attendant insecurities,
with depravity.

For the revolutionary, the field of symbolization is
dominated by the necessity of struggle, which has the
privilege of giving meaning to the world. The figure of the
non-combatant accordingly has no power to intervene in this
field: "civilians" are part of the *matter* of the world, passively
enthralled or enchanted – and so in a manner of speaking
given form - by the state. The task of the revolutionary

vanguard is to break this enchantment by actively resisting the state, besieging it with vexations which will force it to reveal its true oppressive nature. Once this is accomplished, there will be no more "civilians": all will become involved in the political process, on one side or another. But only the disenchanted have agency: it is like a playground game of statues, in which captured players must be tagged by free players before they can move again. The statues cannot free themselves: they must be acted upon before they in their turn can act. Once one has analyzed the positions of the statues, one does not expect them to move around of their own accord.

This tendency of revolutionary vanguards to regard themselves as the only true agents in a situation is illustrated by Meinhof's discussion of the armed robberies committed by the group. Meinhof maintains simultaneously that they carried these robberies out because they needed the money, and that their guilt has not been proven: the police are still trying to "pin" the robberies on them; they are overreacting, given that all they have to go on is a suspicion. It is of course perfectly possible for both of these things to be true at once; but nevertheless a contradiction arises when they are both asserted together by the same speaker in the presence of the same hearer. It is like saying to the detective in a murder case: "you have no evidence that I murdered my wife - which I did in a fit of jealous passion because I had discovered her infidelity". The statement itself can be taken as the very evidence the existence of which it denies.

This type of self-contradiction is known as a *performative* contradiction. Like the record-player-destroying vinyl records of Douglas Hofstadter's *Gödel, Escher, Bach: An Eternal Golden Braid,* which cause the apparatus playing them to produce sound waves that resonate with its mechanism and shake it to pieces, a performatively contradictory statement becomes contradictory only when it is performed, or stated "out loud" in some pragmatic situation. The statement "I am absolutely at a loss for words" is performatively contradictory in any situation in which "I" am the speaker, because of the implicit self-reference: I, who am speaking now, cannot therefore be as dumbstruck as I say I am. But the contradiction in Meinhof'statement regarding the robberies only arises if that statement is made in the hearing of a supposed accuser: "how impertinent of you to accuse me of committing those robberies, which in any case I only carried out because I needed the money".

Now, even if *Das Konzept Stadtguerrilla* had initially only been circulated among comrades, the chances of a copy eventually landing on the desk of some detective must have been fairly high. Let us assume that Meinhof must have been aware of this. To put it another way, there are a number of other hints in the text that suggest that the police are among its implied readers. Take for example the statement of the principle that the militants will not shoot at armed officers who permit them to escape instead of opening fire ("the bull that lets us run, we also let run", which rather suggests a festive Iberian street scene). This hints at the possibility of an unspoken pact of mutual non-violence *between combatants*, in which both sides might refrain - out of professional courtesy, as the old joke about sharks and lawyers has it - from shooting at each other, whilst perhaps continuing to gun down bystanders with remorseless ontological indifference. At the very least, it is readable as an attempt to persuade the vacillating state enforcer, whom Meinhof characterises as a "little man" and a knave of capitalism (*Kapitalistenknecht*), to exercise a prudent discretion in the use of firearms.

Rather than representing it as a lapse in awareness, an accidental giveaway, we should therefore take the contradiction in Meinhof's statement as *feigned*. What it announces to the uniformed eavesdropper is rather the group's complete indifference to his symbolic agency, his participation in the pragmatic situation in which a performative contradiction might arise. The effect is similar to that of talking loudly about someone in the room as if they were not there, seeking to attract their attention precisely so one can refuse to respond to it.

The conviction of Meinhof and her comrades that the situation was ripe for revolutionary intervention was not a response to ubiquitous, catastrophic disorder, but neither did it arise spontaneously in the midst of an otherwise tranquil society. One particular flashpoint was the murder of the student protestor Benno Ohnesorg, savagely beaten and then shot in the head by police during demonstrations against a visit by the Shah of Iran. Gudrun Ensslin's angry declaration, after this outrage, is pivotal: "They'll kill us all. You know what kind of pigs we're up against. This is the Auschwitz generation. You can't argue with the people who made Auschwitz. They have weapons and we haven't. We must arm ourselves!"

This is not exactly an overreaction. It is however less a rational estimation of the magnitude of the hostile forces presented by "the system" than a symbolic putting-to-death of society in general. "Auschwitz" here signifies not only the real threat of state violence, but the foreclosure of negotiation. "You can't argue with the people who made Auschwitz", not only because they are better-armed than you but also because they are beyond the reach of persuasion or polemic, wholly identified with what they *do*: generators of Auschwitz, "the Auschwitz generation". Once the state is identified, via such representative authority figures as the police and the "older generation" of one's parents and teachers, as the possibility of recurrence of Auschwitz (and all of its acts, from the suppression of student demonstrations to the saturation-bombing of Vietnam, as smaller or greater Auschwitzes), the ground is prepared for a revolutionary ethics of secession.

What is political engagement for those under the enchantment of the state? In thought, it is the browsing of newspapers; in deed, the conduct of "high-profile" media campaigns. What the papers say, and what one says about it in one's turn, constitutes the fabric of "political" discourse, the world of current affairs. What "The Concept of the Urban Guerrilla" metonymises as "the Springer press" is this manufactured un-world, a simulacrum which absorbs and sublimates political discontent, refashioning it as opinion. For Meinhof, herself a successful journalist prior to her conversion to the cause of armed struggle, the entire world of political discussion, from the bully-pulpit oration of newspaper columnists to the obscure and earnest analyses of leftist groups, is simply a means by which potentially revolutionary displeasure is cathected, dissipated, drawn off and recirculated. The passage from concerned leftist political discourse to concerted militant activism is a passage from that which soothes, placates and mollifies to that which concentrates displeasure and directs it towards its source: a militant dysphoria.

We may therefore understand the urban guerrilla's secession from the state as involving two symbolic gestures. The first of these is the freezing of the state, fixing it to a single figure guilty of a defining outrage for which it is eternally responsible, and the recurrence of which it continually threatens. Doris Lessing's hapless British activists in *The Good Terrorist* all seem to have a story to tell about their unhappy childhoods, which perhaps serves in lieu of larger-scale social trauma. The goal of one is simply to "put an end to it all so that children don't have a bad time, the way I did". As Alice, the novel's curiously child-like protagonist, bitterly observes: "I've had all the bloody unhappy childhoods I'm going to listen to…Communes. Squats. If you don't take care, that's what they become – people sitting around discussing their shitty childhoods". The actions of the state are framed as repetitions of a primal scene, a scene which paradoxically creates the activist dedicated to eliminating the very possibility of its occurrence.

The second gesture which effects the militant's separation from the state is the refusal of all palliatives, in particular those which assist in the sublimation of anger and the relief of dissatisfaction. Monika Berberich recalls that the men and women of the Red Army Fraction would routinely call each other "silly bitch" and "tosser": "we were trying to transcend bourgeois language, which could be rather indirect. We didn't want to talk around things any more. We just wanted to tell it like it is". This is above all a refusal to be symbolically integrated, to be part of a common conversation in which what "everybody says" and what "everybody knows" are effectively co-extensive. The RAF sought a knowledge inaccessible through the exchange of ready opinions, a knowledge of how things really stood as opposed to how they were positioned within the space of representation. They conceived of obscene speech and violent action as tools for excavating reality.

The political conflicts in which the RAF sought to intervene were real and serious. They regarded themselves as Western partisans for the third-world enemies of imperialism, engaged in the same struggle – and on the same side – as the Vietcong and Che Guevara. They believed that it was necessary to counter dispel the illusion of invulnerability created by Western affluence backed by American superpower, to open up a space for action by demonstrating that it was possible for an armed resistance to operate even in the midst of the most technologically advanced security apparatus in the world. Their aim was quite simply to punch a hole through the consensus reality of their society. But in order to conceive of doing this, they had to radically simplify their vision of how that society worked, treating every manifestation of power or authority as an emanation from the same dark star. They also had to withdraw, not only from the tittle-tattle of parliamentary correspondents and the manufactured talking points of the yellow press, but also from any engagement with their society's symbolic order beyond unilateral posturing. Perhaps the definitive form of RAF utterance is the taunting rhetorical question: "Did the pigs really think that we would let Comrade Baader languish in prison for 2 or 3 years?"

In the political world of the RAF, a world locked in conflict, the indiscernible agency of elderly librarians and other non-combatants, "collateral damage" in the grand struggle between imperialism and its enemies, could only manifest itself as contingency and mishap: something that inexplicably got in the way. But the secret of the cold world is that there is something moving in its icy wastes, something astir in its gloomy forests. The statues blink and change positions in the night. Coleridge wrote of the "secret ministry of frost" that worked in the depths of midnight, hanging icicles under the eaves of the house: even in the frozen world there is continual change, the accumulation of numberless imperceptibly tiny changes. This hidden agency is most often conceived as supernatural, since it lies outside of the normal realm of human action and symbolisation; but in fact it is nature itself, nature as the unconscious of human reality: the "it" traversing the dejected "I". Late black metal, in its vertiginous mortal despair, is more sensitive to the secret ministries of this unconscious than the unreflective activism of the self-styled urban guerrilla. But these cannot be the only choices.

The cold world is a world whose active principle has ceased to function. In the vitalist's cold world, the distinction between living and dead matter collapses: the world *is dead*, and life appears within it as an irrational persistence, an insupportable excrescence. In aesthetics, the cold world is that world in which matter is no longer given form by imagination, and ceases to cohere into the "higher" truth of an aesthetic unity: it loses its integrity, becoming a waste ground of disconnected phenomena, "a heap of broken images". In the cold world of the hedonist, the distinction between pleasure and displeasure loses pertinence: there is no enjoyment to be had anywhere within it, and the pleasures of others are scorned as guilty and contemptible. The hedonism of West German society arrived at its terminus in the brain of Ulrike Meinhof, and her war against that society was a desperate attempt to recover the reality it had occluded.

When the fundamental distinction of a world collapses in this way, something becomes visible that was formerly indiscernible: the "inorganic life" of anonymous natural process; the archipelago of local truths woven out of amorous encounters; the secret enjoyment of others which is never fully apparent in their public pursuit of happiness. What was it that moved poor Linke into the path of the guerrillas' gunfire? Let us close with this conjecture: it was neither bravery nor blind panic, but desire to be in on the act; to die if needs be, but in any event to touch on the real.

Further Reading

Badiou, Alain, *Theoretical Writings*, trans. and ed. Ray Brassier and Alberto Toscano. London: Continuum, 2006.

De Man, Paul, *The Rhetoric of Romanticism*. New York, Columbia University Press, 1986.

Lessing, Doris, *The Good Terrorist*. London: Jonathan Cape, 1985.

Martin, Robert B., *Gerard Manley Hopkins: A Very Private Life*. London: Putnam, 1991.

Moynihan, Martin and Didrik Søderlind., *Lords of Chaos: The Bloody Rise of the Satanic Metal Underground*. Los Angeles: Feral House, 2003.

Murdoch, Iris, *The Flight From The Enchanter*, intr. Patricia Duncker. London: Vintage 2000.

Vague, Tom, Televisionaries: The Red Army Faction Story. London: AK Press, 1994.

Further Listening

Codeine, *The White Birch*. CD. Seattle: Sub Pop, 1994.

Darkthrone, *Transilvanian Hunger*. CD. West Yorkshire: Peaceville, 2001.

Xasthur, *Subliminal Genocide*. CD. Boston: Hydra Head, 2006.

Nortt, *Galgenfrist*. CD. Italy: Avantgarde, 2008.

Contemporary culture has eliminated both the concept of the public and the figure of the intellectual. Former public spaces – both physical and cultural – are now either derelict or colonized by advertising. A cretinous anti-intellectualism presides, cheerled by expensively educated hacks in the pay of multinational corporations who reassure their bored readers that there is no need to rouse themselves from their interpassive stupor. The informal censorship internalized and propagated by the cultural workers of late capitalism generates a banal conformity that the propaganda chiefs of Stalinism could only ever have dreamt of imposing. Zero Books knows that another kind of discourse – intellectual without being academic, popular without being populist – is not only possible: it is already flourishing, in the regions beyond the striplit malls of so-called mass media and the neurotically bureaucratic halls of the academy. Zero is committed to the idea of publishing as a making public of the intellectual. It is convinced that in the unthinking, blandly consensual culture in which we live, critical and engaged theoretical reflection is more important than ever before.